CALLING ALL SOCIAL WORKERS!

THIS TOTALLY RELATABLE COLORING BOOK WAS MADE JUST FOR YOU

INSIDE THIS BOOK YOU WILL FIND 20 MANDALAS FOR YOU TO SIT BACK AND COLOR

EACH ONE CONTAINS A PROBLEM OR QUOTE THAT YOU SHOULD DEFINITELY BE ABLE TO RELATE TO!

HAPPY COLORING

COLORING CREW

YOU
CAN'T FIX
CRAZY BUT
YOU CAN
DOCUMENT
IT

COLORING CREW

WHEN YOU'RE AT A HOME VISIT AND THEIR PET IS SO CUTE THAT YOU CAN'T FOCUS

COLORING
CREW

YOU
CAN'T
SCARE ME
I'M A SOCIAL
WORKER

COLORING
CREW

WHEN YOUR FRIEND CALLS YOU BUT YOU'VE ALREADY ANSWERED THE PHONE 1000 TIMES THAT DAY

COLORING
CREW

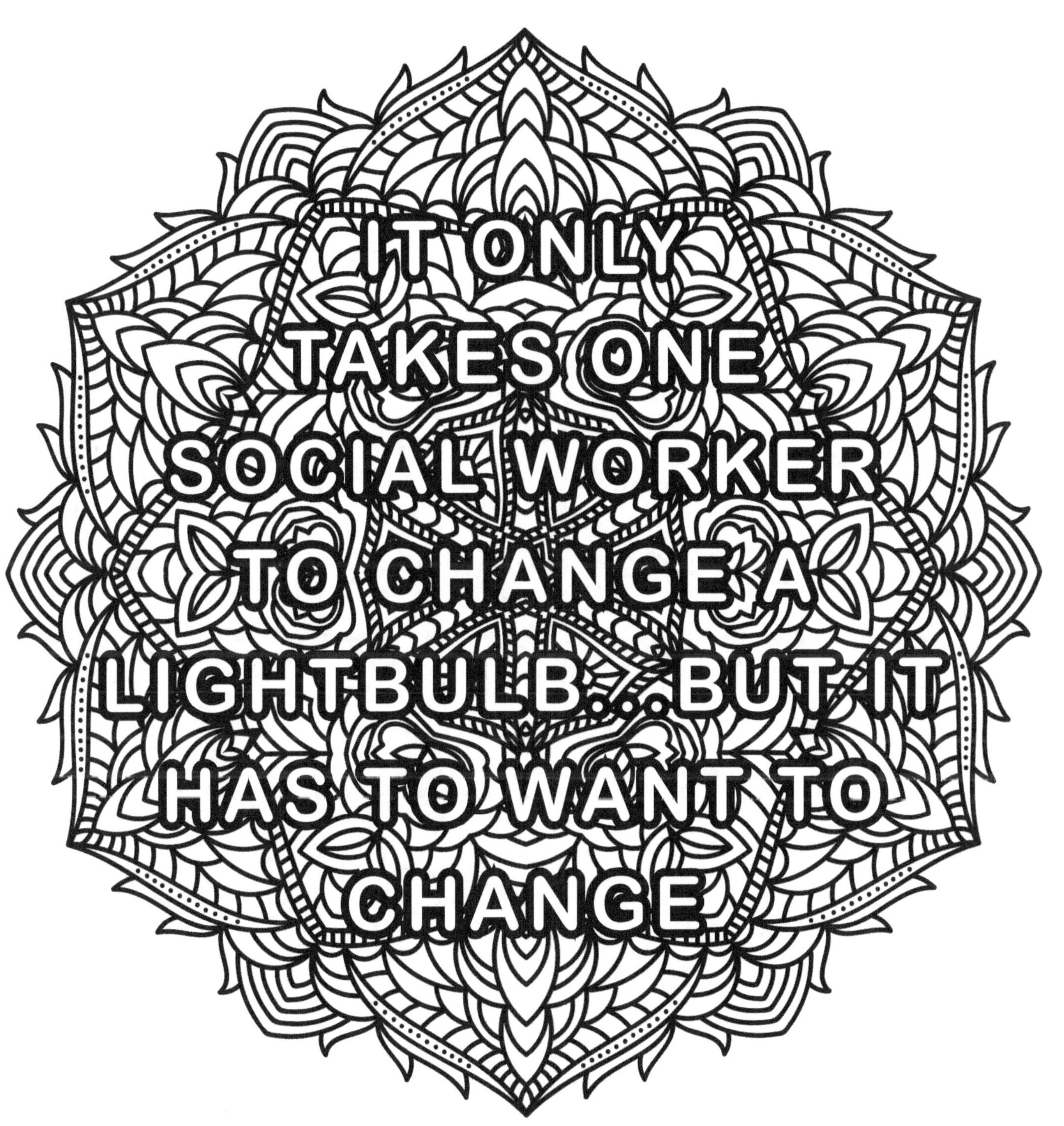

IT ONLY TAKES ONE SOCIAL WORKER TO CHANGE A LIGHTBULB...BUT IT HAS TO WANT TO CHANGE

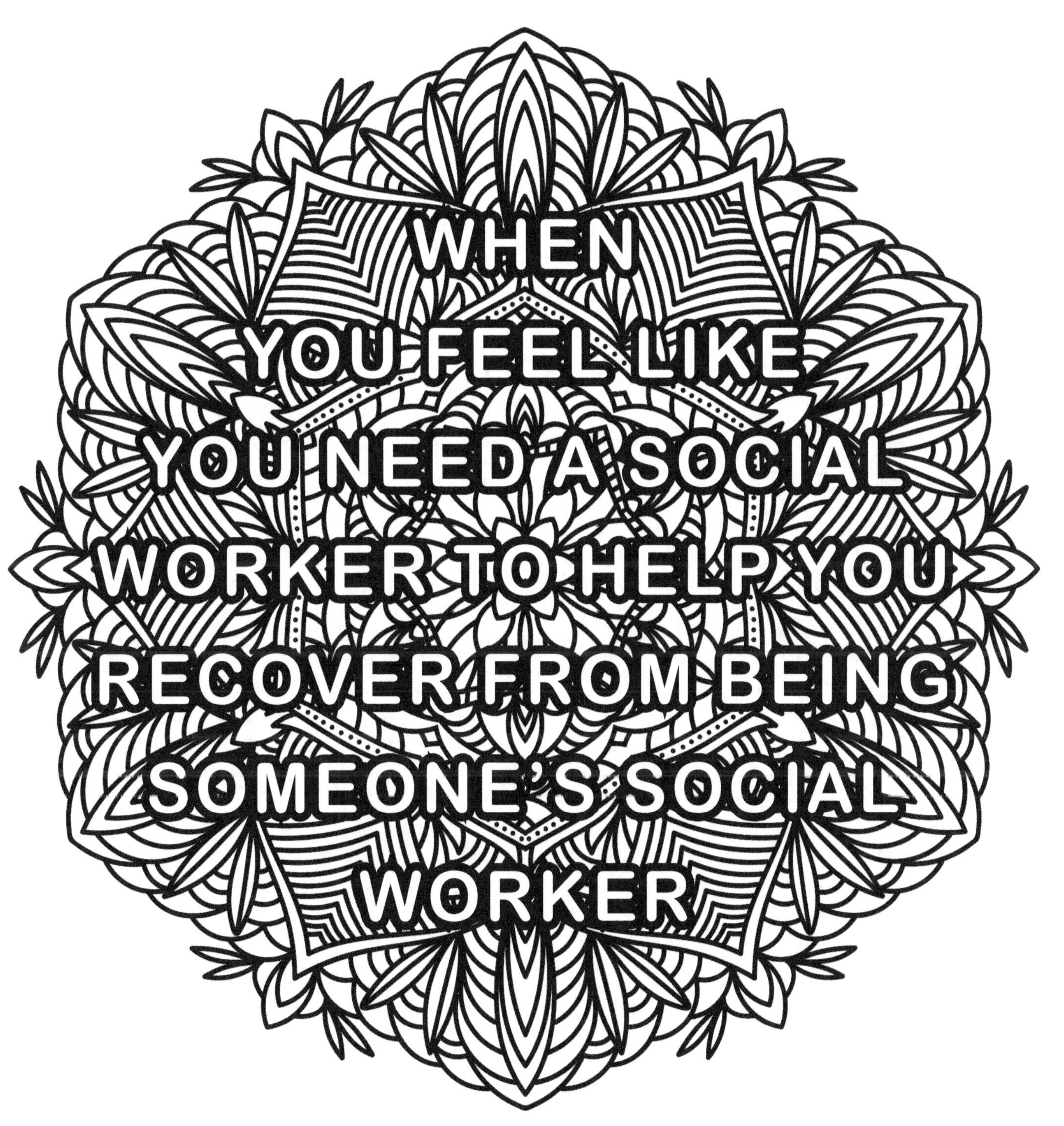

WHEN
YOU FEEL LIKE
YOU NEED A SOCIAL
WORKER TO HELP YOU
RECOVER FROM BEING
SOMEONE'S SOCIAL
WORKER

COLORING
CREW

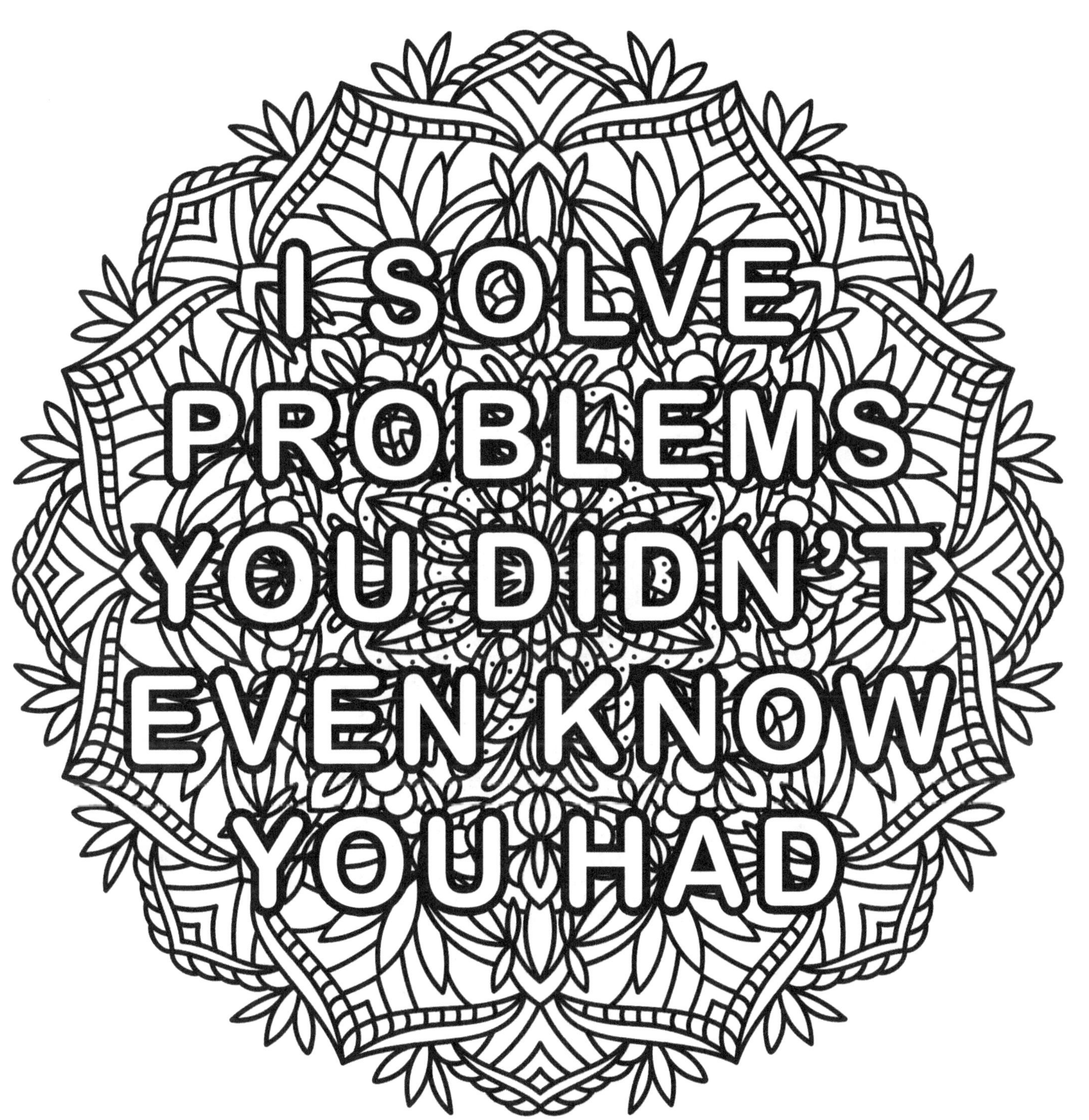
I SOLVE
PROBLEMS
YOU DIDN'T
EVEN KNOW
YOU HAD

COLORING
CREW

IM A
SOCIAL
WORKER
BECAUSE MIRACLE
WORKER ISN'T AN
OFFICIAL JOB
TITLE

COLORING
CREW

IF AT
FIRST YOU
DON'T SUCCEED...
DO WHAT YOUR
SOCIAL WORKER
TOLD YOU TO DO
THE FIRST
TIME

I'M NOT JUDGING YOU I I JUST HAVE EXCELENT ASSESSMENT SKILLS

COLORING
CREW

SOCIAL
WORK IS LIKE
PEEING YOURSELF
IN DARK PANTS, YOU
GET A WARM FEELING
BUT NOBODY ELSE
NOTICES

PLEASE
DON'T CONFUSE
YOUR GOOGLE
SEARCH WITH MY
QUALIFICATIONS

COLORING
CREW

A SOCIAL WORKER'S MIND IS LIKE A BROWSER WITH 283 TABS OPEN AT ALL TIMES

"I DO THIS FOR THE MONEY"
SAID NO SOCIAL WORKER EVER

I'VE
PROBABLY
ALREADY SEEN
IT, HEARD IT AND
WRITTEN A GOAL
FOR IT

DON'T
MAKE
ME USE
MY SOCIAL
WORKER
VOICE ON
YOU

COLORING
CREW

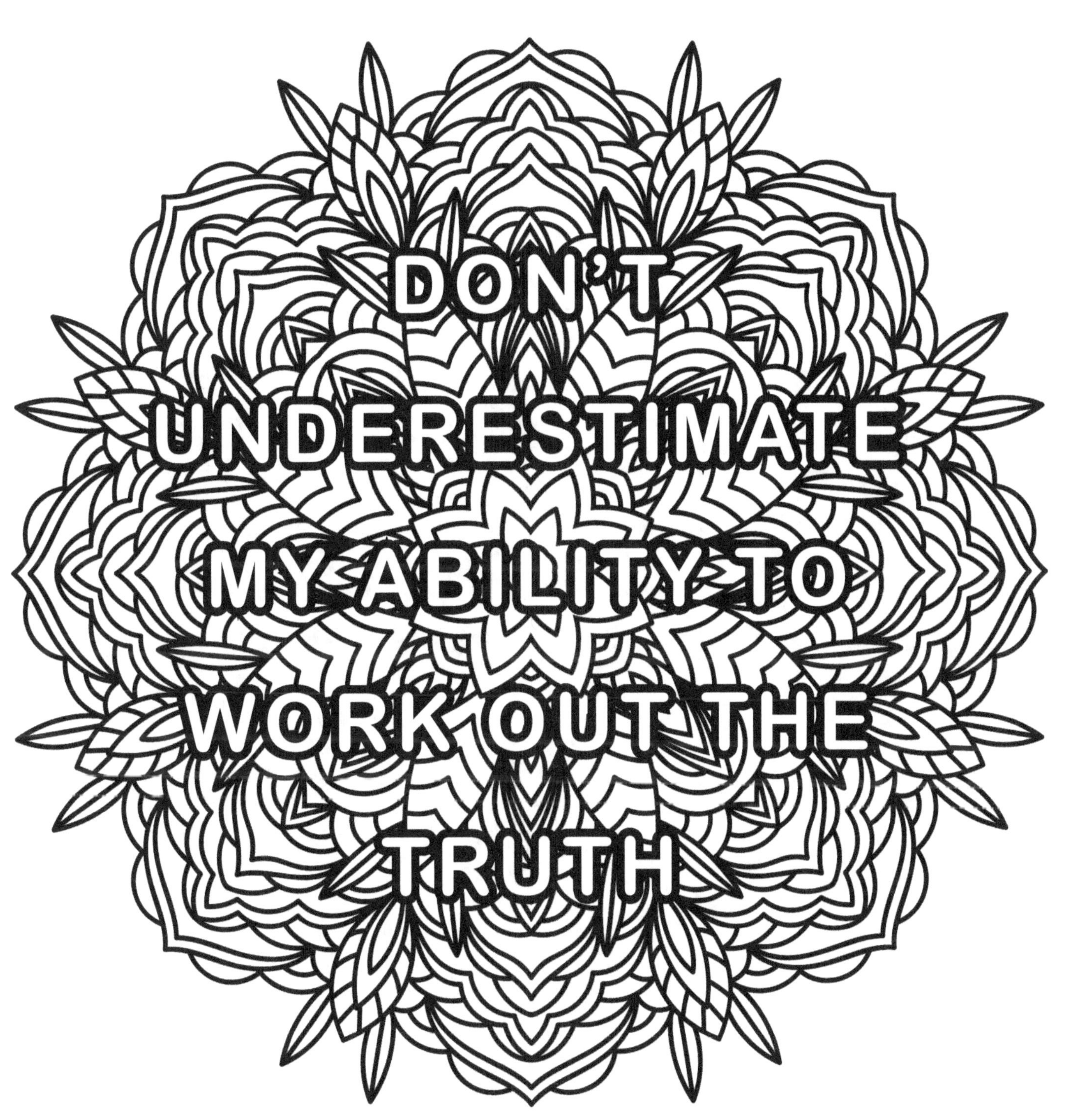

DON'T
UNDERESTIMATE
MY ABILITY TO
WORK OUT THE
TRUTH

NO I
DON'T TAKE
PEOPLE'S KIDS
AWAY FOR A
LIVING

THAT MOMENT
WHEN YOU REALIZE
HOW MANY PEOPLE
ARE WALKING AROUND
UNMEDICATED AND
UNSUPERVISED

OH
YOU HAVE
PROBLEMS?
WELL I HAVE 100
OTHER PEOPLE'S
PROBLEMS

COLOR TEST
PAGE

THANKS!
WE HOPE YOU HAD FUN!

IF YOU LIKED THIS BOOK THEN YOU YOU CAN
VIEW OUR FULL RANGE OF HILARIOUS ADULT
COLORING BOOKS BY GOING TO AMAZON AND
SEARCHING FOR "COLORING CREW" AND THEN
CLICKING ON OUR AUTHOR PAGE.

THANKS AGAIN!